Stickers 1

Page 3

Page 5

Page 7

Page 9

Page 11

Page 13

T0046146

Page
15

Page
17

Page
19

Page
21

Page
23

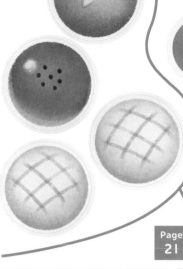

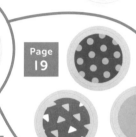

Thumbelina .....

The Three Bears .....

Cinderella

Little Red Riding Hood ....

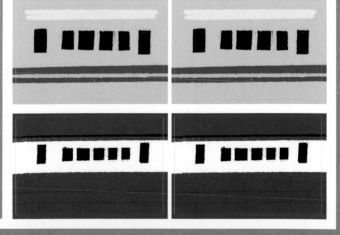

Page
25

Page
27

Page
29

Page
35

Page
33

Page
31

FRUIT
SNACKS

Reward Stickers

Stickers 4

Page 37

Page 39

Page 41

Page 43

Page 45

Reward Stickers

Page 47

Page 49

Page 51

Page 53

FARM

Reward Stickers

Page
55

Page
57

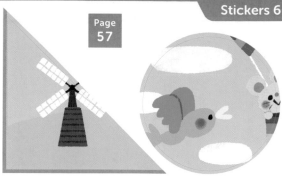

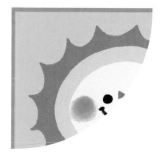

Page
59

Page
61

POLICE

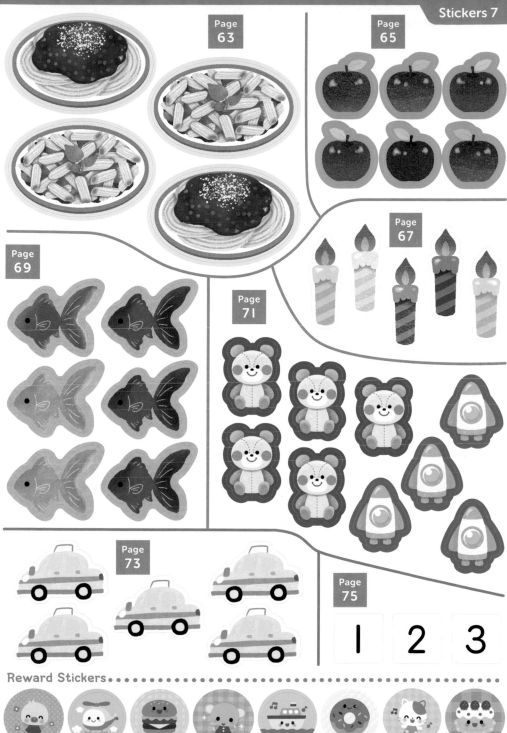

Stickers 7

Page 63

Page 65

Page 67

Page 69

Page 71

Page 73

Page 75

1 2 3

Reward Stickers

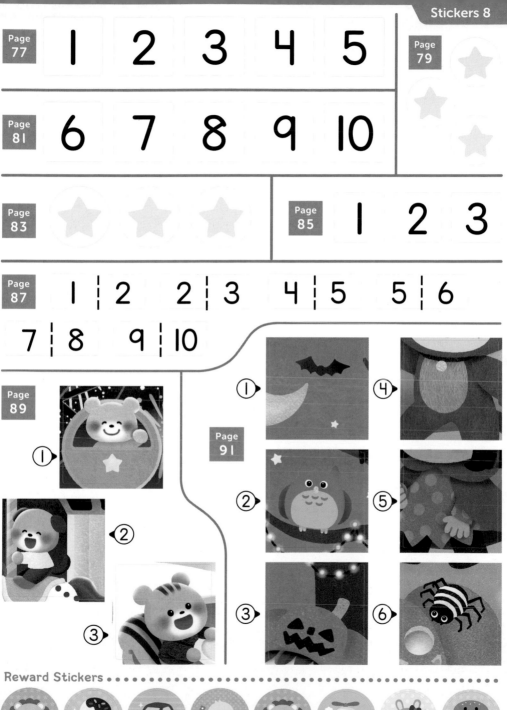

Note to Parents

1) The activities in this book are at an appropriate developmental level so your child can do them independently. But don't hesitate to help them! When parents are involved in the learning process, it increases a child's intellectual curiosity and creates a more effective, supportive learning environment.

2) To support your child's learning, review the **"To Parents"** section featured below the instructions. These tips offer effective ways to explain the activity to your child.

3) Besides the **sticker activities**, this book includes **additional activities** that use pencils and crayons to develop school readiness skills. By alternating between the sticker pages and the other activities, children will learn to classify by color, shape, and size while boosting observation, self-confidence, self-esteem, vocabulary, creativity, and problem-solving skills.

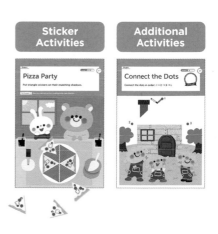

4) When your child finishes the additional activities, let them choose a **reward sticker** to put on the page. Be sure to also praise your child's good work! Be specific with your praise, saying something like, "You did a good job counting!" or "You were very patient!"

Counting 1 to 10

1

2

3

4

5

6

7

8

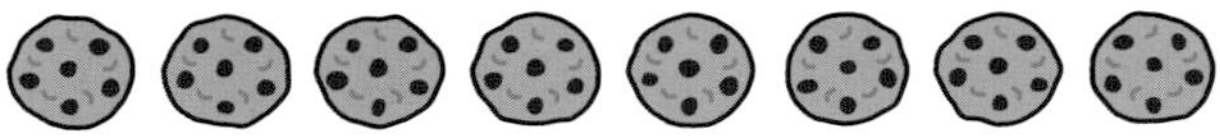

9

10

Yellow Chicks

Put yellow chick stickers on the grass.

Name the Color

Say the color of each stuffed animal.

Good job!

To Parents Once your child can say each color, have them say both the color and name of the toy, such as red bear and yellow bunny.

yellow

red

blue

green

white

black

Busy Cars

Put red car stickers on the road.

Find the Blue Animals

Find the blue sea animals and point to them.

Good job!

Fresh Vegetables

Find and add stickers to complete each vegetable.

To Parents When your child is finished, say the color and name of each vegetable, such as red tomato, purple eggplant, and yellow corn.

Yummy Ice Cream Cones

Find the ice cream cone that matches the one in the box and point to it.

Good job!

To Parents First ask your child to name the color of each ice cream cone, then find one that matches the example.

Find this ice cream cone!

Cheerful Flowers

Put blue flower stickers on the tables.

To Parents | This activity allows your child to practice applying stickers to a limited space.

Color Match

Good job!

Draw a line from ● to ● to match the color in each circle to the color of each animal.

To Parents Once your child can connect the lines, say both the color and animal, such as white bear and gray elephant.

Summer Fun

Put circle stickers on their matching shadows.

To Parents Encourage your child to find the large and small circles before adding the stickers.

Color Match

Draw lines from ⭐ to ⚫.

Good job!

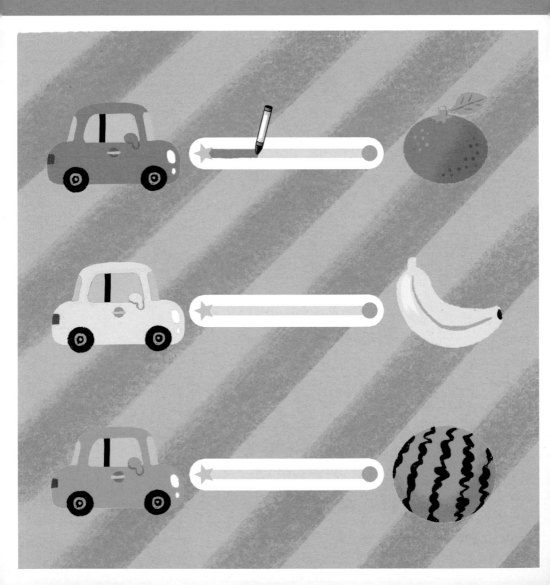

Around and Around

Put circle stickers on their matching shadows.

To Parents | All circles are the same size. It is okay if your child adds the stickers and they are not aligned with the shadows. They will gradually be able to achieve this.

Vegetable Stand

Find the green vegetables and point to them.

Good job!

cucumber   eggplant   carrot   green pepper

Freshly Baked Bread

Put circle stickers on their matching shadows.

Clothes Match

Find the outfit that matches the one in the box and point to it.

Good job!

Find this outfit!

Beautiful Butterfly

Put circle stickers on their matching shadows
to complete the butterfly.

To Parents | The circle stickers are now a little smaller. Tell your child to make a beautiful butterfly and encourage them to put stickers wherever they like.

Find the Same Giraffe

Find the giraffe that matches the one in the box and point to it.

Good job!

To Parents | Encourage your child to pay attention to the giraffe's pattern and color. Ask them to point to the yellow giraffes, then have them notice the different patterns on their bodies.

Find this giraffe!

Cheerful Pattern

Put circle stickers on their matching shadows to finish the pattern.

Draw Curved Lines

Good job!

Draw lines from ⭐ to ●.

Favorite Stories

Put rectangle stickers on their matching shadows.

To Parents | Encourage your child to put stickers on the gray squares. If this is difficult, help them by placing one corner of the sticker down first and adjust from there.

Name the Shape

Trace each shape with your finger.
Then, say the shape's name.

Good job!

circle

rectangle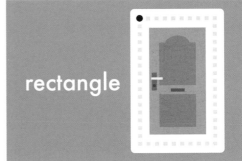

square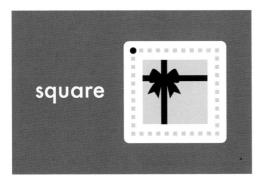

diamond

triangle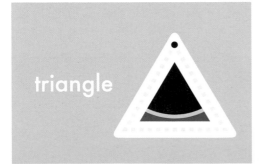

star

Colorful Trains

Put rectangle stickers on their matching shadows.

To Parents | Use the train's colors and patterns to identify the matching train car stickers.

Toy Store

Find the circle-shaped toys and point to them.

Good job!

Candy Cottage

Put square and rectangle stickers on their matching shadows.

Draw a Circle

Draw a line from ⭐ to ⬤.

Good job!

To Parents | If your child has difficulty tracing, put your hand on theirs to help them draw.

Sweet Treats

Put rectangle stickers on their matching shadows.

Party Time

Good job!

Find the square-shaped presents and point to them.

Rainbow Castle

Put square and rectangle stickers on their matching shadows.

Through to the Park

Draw a line from  to .

Good job!

To Parents | Encourage your child to stop drawing when they need to change direction, then start again.

Colors and Patterns

Find and add stickers to complete each animal.

To Parents | Make sure to put the cow pattern sticker in the right direction.

Treasure Chests

Good job!

Draw a line from ➡ to ➡ through each rectangular treasure chest.

To Parents | If your child has difficulty drawing long lines, encourage them to take a break when they reach each treasure chest and then start again.

Happy Birthday

Put triangle stickers on their matching shadows.

To Parents | It might be difficult for your child to place triangle-shaped stickers. Put one corner down first and adjust it from there.

My Neighborhood

Good job!

Find the houses with a triangle-shaped roof and point to them.

Cruising Sailboats

Put triangle stickers on their matching shadows.

Happy Hats

Find the triangle-shaped hats and point to them.

Good job!

Pizza Party

Put triangle stickers on their matching shadows.

To Parents | Make sure each pizza slice is pointing in the right direction.

Spot the Differences

Find two differences between the top and bottom picture.

Level 1 ★☆☆   38

Good job!

To Parents | The star on the boy's shirt and the triangle block are different in these pictures.

Top

Bottom

My Community

Put triangle stickers on their matching shadows.

Connect the Dots

Good job!

Connect the dots in order: I → 2 → 3 → I.

Fruit Snacks

Put fruit stickers on their matching shadows.

To Parents | Guide your child to match the stickers in order from easiest to hardest: melon, orange, watermelon, apple.

Spot the Differences

Find three differences between the top and bottom picture.

Level 2 ★★☆   42

Good job!

To Parents | The squirrel, bird, and cat's food are different in these pictures.

Top

Bottom

Animals in the Zoo

Put animal stickers on their matching shadows.

To Parents | Ask your child to identify the animal shadows. Have them pay attention to animal features such as the elephant's trunk, the panda's ears, and the lion's mane.

Lunchtime

Find the food that matches the one in the box and point to it.

Good job!

Find this food!

Swimming Sea Animals

Put sea animal stickers on their matching shadows.

Animal Match

Draw a line from ● to ● to match each animal with its face.

Good job!

Petting Zoo

Put animal stickers on their matching shadows.

Frosty Maze

Draw a line from ➡ to ➡.

Good job!

Favorite Toy

Put toy stickers on their matching shadows.

Draw a Star

Draw a line from ⭐ to ●.

Good job!

Amusement Park

Put stickers on their matching shadows.

Spot the Differences

Find two differences between the top and bottom picture.

Good job!

To Parents | The girl's outfit and the boy's pants are different in the pictures.

Top

Bottom

Cool Clothes

Put clothing stickers on their matching shadows.

To Parents Put one part of the sticker on first, such as the sleeve, and adjust from there.

Spot the Differences

Find two differences between the top and bottom picture.

To Parents | The lion's mane, the purple balloon, and the merry-go-round are different in the pictures.

Animal Puzzles

Put stickers on their matching shadows.
Complete the picture so it matches the example.

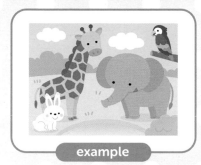

example

ZOO

Color the Stars

Good job!

Color the stars with your favorite color.

To Parents | Color the star pattern with your child. It is okay if your child colors outside of the stars.

Up and Away!

Put stickers on their matching shadows.
Complete the picture so it matches the example.

To Parents | Align the circle sticker with the mouse's face and the bird's tail.

example

Color the Diamonds

Color the diamond shapes with your favorite color.

Good job!

Playground Puzzle

Put stickers on their matching shadows.
Complete the picture so it matches the example.

example

Match the Vehicle Parts

Draw a line from ● to ● to match each vehicle with its part.

Good job!

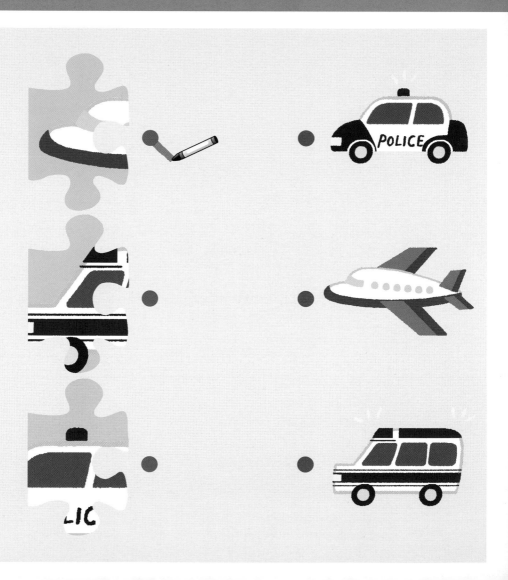

Busy Vehicles Puzzle

Put stickers on their matching shadows.
Complete the picture so it matches the example.

To Parents Following the example, have your child pay attention to the color and shape of each vehicle.

example

Collect the Puzzle Pieces

Draw a line from ➡ to ➡ and collect the puzzle pieces on the path.

Good job!

Dining Out

Put a sticker on the place mats so each animal
has a plate of pasta.

To Parents | The number of animals and plates of pasta is the same. This is called one-to-one correspondence.
After each animal has a plate of pasta, praise your child by saying, "Good job."

Favorite Things

Draw a line from ➡ to ➡ and collect the cat's favorite things on the path.

Apple Orchard

Put two apple stickers on each tree.

Find the Number I

Find the number I and trace it with
your favorite color.

Good job!

Birthday Candles

Put candle stickers on each cake to match the age of each child.

Two years old

Three years old

Find the Number 2

Find the number 2 and trace it with
your favorite color.

Good job!

Count the Goldfish

Put goldfish stickers in each tank so it matches the number on the left.

one
1

two
2

three
3

Find the Number 3

Find the number 3 and trace it with your favorite color.

Good job!

Count the Toys

Put toy stickers in the blue and red toy boxes
so they match the number on the left.

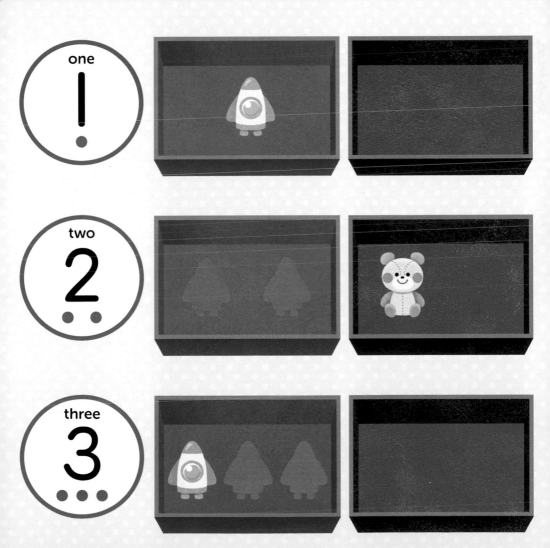

Playful Pets

Count the dogs. Then, color the same number of ◯ with your favorite color.

To Parents | If this seems difficult, draw circles around the dogs and then draw lines to connect them to the circles below.

Taxis in the City

Count the taxis. Then, put the matching number of taxi stickers in the box below.

Level 2 ★★☆ 74

Count the Sweets

Count the chocolate chip cookies, cherry cookies, and candies. Then, color the same number of ◯ as each sweet with your favorite color.

Good job!

To Parents   This activity practices identifying and counting objects that are similar shapes. If this seems difficult, color each row of circles with a different color.

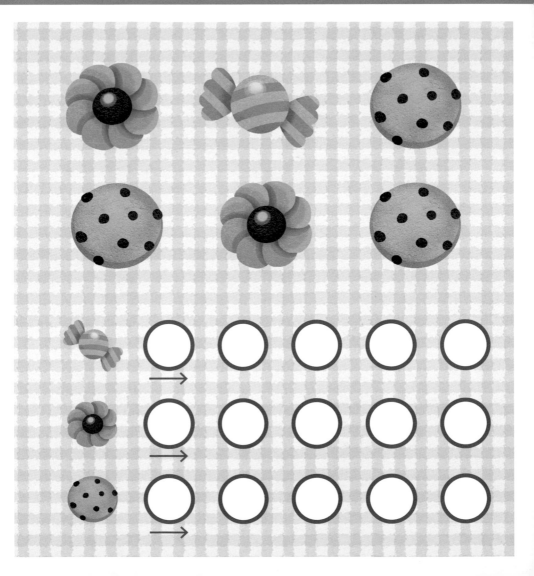

Zoom Zoom!

Count the kids on each ride.
Then, put the matching number sticker on ☐.

Count the School Supplies

Good job!

Count the scissors, crayons, and rolls of tape. Then, color the same number of ○ as each school supply with your favorite color.

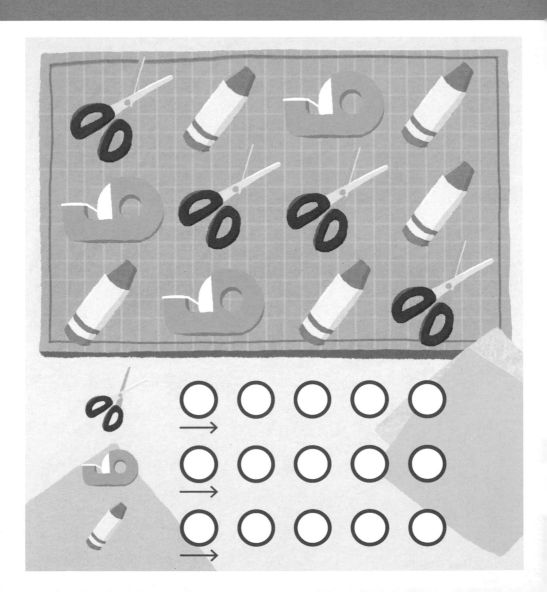

Adventure Park Rides

Count the kids on each ride.
Then, put the matching number sticker on ☐.

To Parents　Tell your child that the kids are grouped by rides, such as the airplanes and teacups.

Which Is More?

Follow the path from → to →. Always go in the direction of the larger number of flowers.

Good job!

To Parents | Count the number of white flowers with your child at each junction, asking your child which is more every time. Repeatedly asking which is more will help them learn the rule.

Which Is More?

Put a star sticker next to the larger number of mice, cars, and cupcakes.

Which Is More?

Draw a line from ➡ to ➡. Always go in
the direction of the larger number of flowers.

Good job!

Count the Balloons

Count the balloons in each bunch.
Then, put the matching number sticker in the box.

Numbers and Trains

Count the trains in each group.
Then, draw a line to the matching number.

Good job!

 1

3

2

2

3

1

Which Is More?

Put a star sticker next to the larger number of birds, cars, and doughnuts.

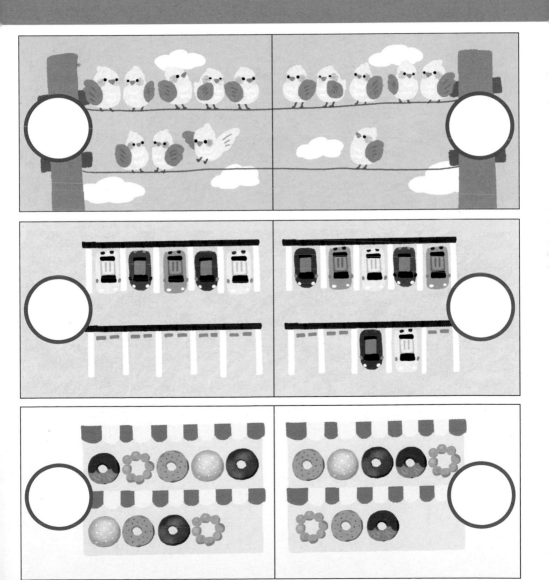

Color by Number

Color the number 3 in black.

Good job!

Number in Order

The numbers are in order from I to 3. Put number stickers in the blank spaces to fill in the train cars.

Color the Chicks

Good job!

Color the chicks with your favorite color.
Then, trace each number.

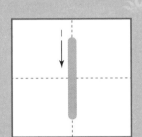

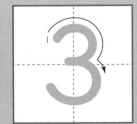

Number in Order

Put number stickers in the blank spaces so they are in order from 1 to 10.

To Parents | Before starting this activity, visit page 2 and count aloud from 1 to 10 with your child.

Match the Numbers

Draw a line from ● to ● to match the number of objects and stars. Then, draw a line from ● to ● to match the stars with the same number.

Good job!

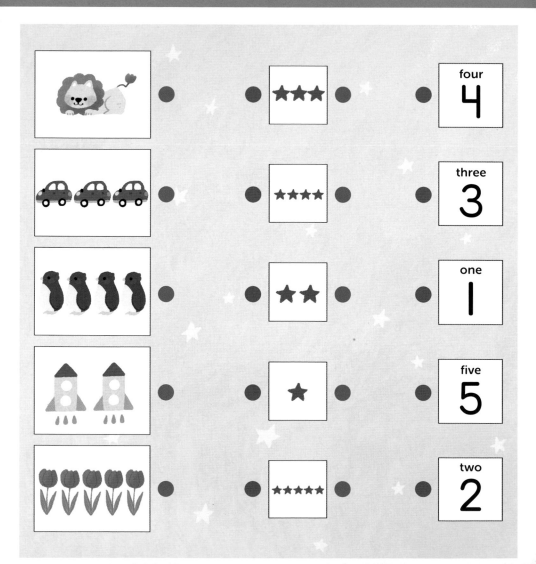

Amusement Park Puzzle

Match the number on the sticker to the number in the gray box. Add the stickers to complete the fun scene.

Match the Numbers

Draw a line from ● to ● to match the number of objects and flowers. Then, draw a line from ● to ● to match the flowers with the same number.

Good job!

seven
7

nine
9

six
6

ten
10

eight
8

Halloween Night Puzzle

Match the number on the sticker to the number in the gray box. Add the stickers to complete the spooky scene.

Which Is More?

Count the dogs, collars, and dog food.
Which is more than the number of dogs—
the collars or the dog food?

Good job!

Connect the Dots

Connect the dots in order from I to IO.

Good job!

To Parents | Before starting this activity, visit page 2 and count aloud from I to IO with your child.

Which Is More?

Follow the path from ➡ to ➡.
Always go in the direction of the larger number.

Good job!

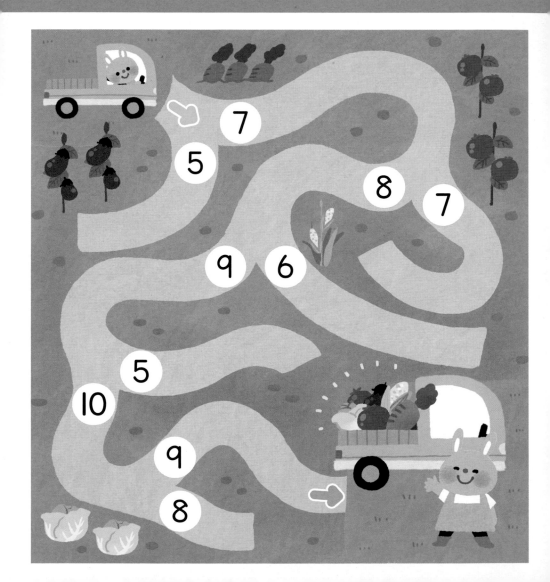

Trace the Numbers

Trace each number.

Good job!

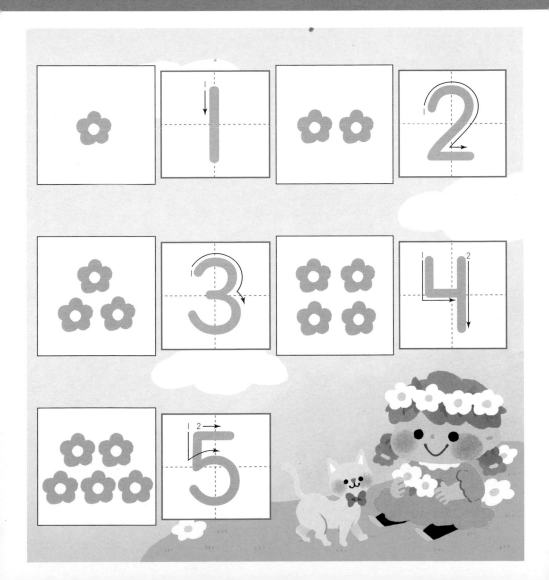

Trace the Numbers

Trace each number.

Good job!

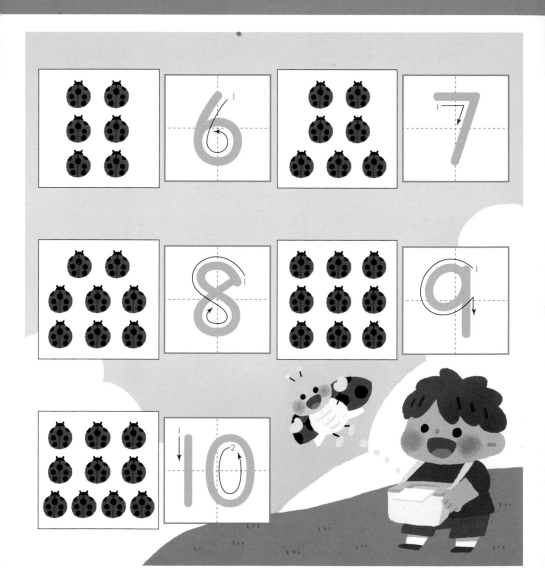